AF094494

This Handwriting Notebook
Belongs To:

A

A is For

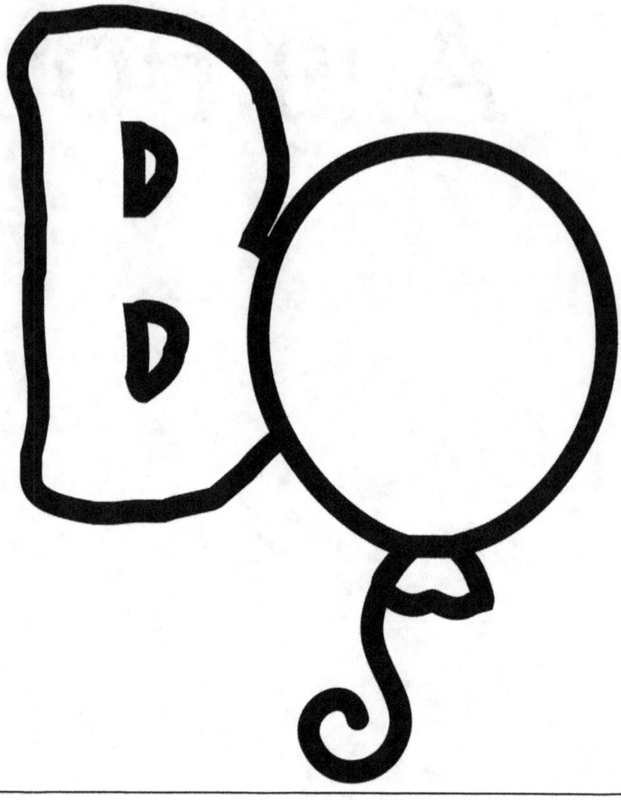

B

B is For

C is For

D

D is For

E

E is For

F is For

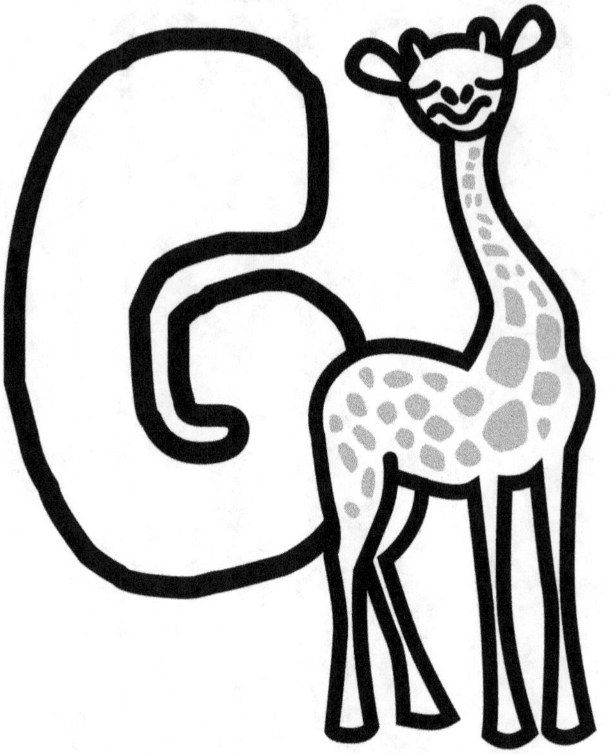

G

G is For

H

H is For

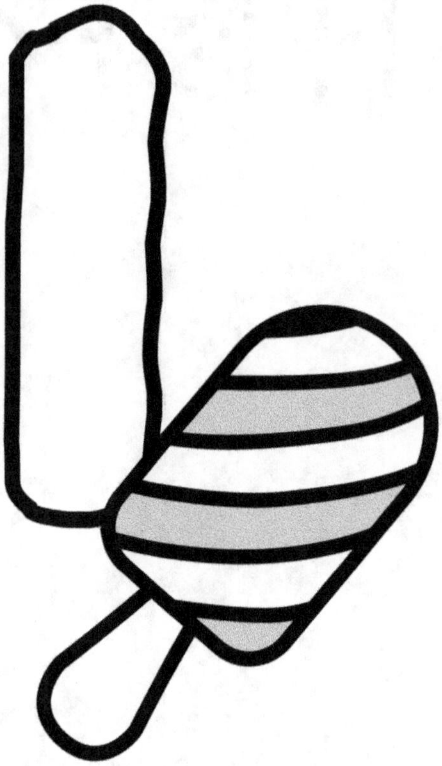

I is For

J

J is For

K

K is For

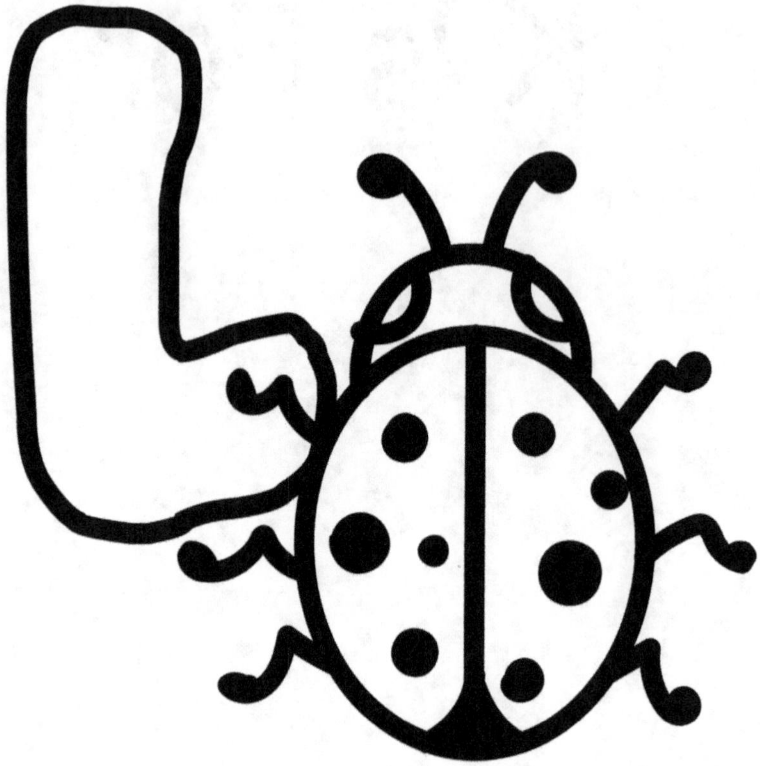

L

L is For

M

M is For

N

N is For

O

O is For

P

P is For

Q is For

R

R is For

S

S is For

T

T is For

U

U is For

v

V is For

W

W is For

X

X is For

Y

Y is For

Z

Z is For

www.ingramcontent.com/pod-product-compliance
Lightning Source LLC
LaVergne TN
LVHW060158080526
838202LV00052B/4163